More Secret Girls' Business

Written by
Heather Anderson
Fay Angelo
Rose Stewart

Illustrated by
Jeff Taylor

The whole story about important girls' business

SGB Publishing Pty Ltd

CONTENTS

- **4** People grow and change all through their lives
- **6** From a girl to a woman
- **8** About puberty
- **9** When will it happen?
- **10** Some changes which happen during puberty
- **12** Hormone levels change
- **14** Hair in different places
- **16** Pimples
- **18** Smelling nice
- **20** Breasts
- **22** Checking breasts
- **23** Bras and Camis
- **24** Changes down below
- **28** How babies are made
- **30** Why do girls have periods?
- **32** Signs that your period may start soon
- **34** How will you know when you get your period? What is your period like?
- **36** How will you feel around the time of your period?
- **37** What can help?
- **38** Getting ready

40	Using pads
42	About tampons
44	How to use a tampon
46	Mood swings
48	These things might help
50	Friends, boyfriends, girlfriends
52	Private moments
54	Masturbation
56	Your Body – Your Rights
58	Feeling good about your body
60	Looking your best
64	Hints for mums, dads, and other significant adults

People grow and change

all through their lives

From a girl to a woman

In your life, there are times when your body changes a lot.

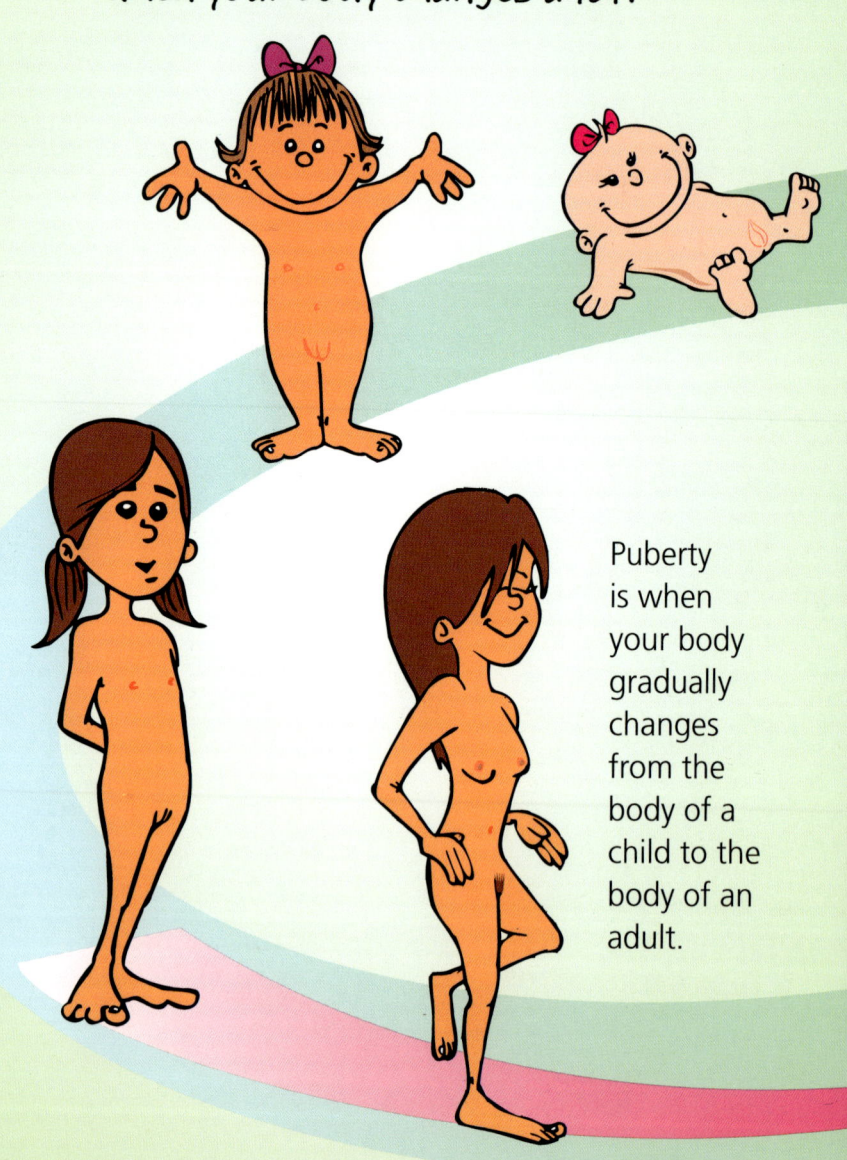

Puberty is when your body gradually changes from the body of a child to the body of an adult.

7

About puberty

Puberty changes the way our bodies look and work, and the way we think and feel.

It prepares a girl's body for having a baby some time in the future, if she chooses.

When will it happen?

Puberty can happen earlier for some and later for others. When your body is the right size and shape for you it will begin to change.

Everyone is different and that's OK.

Some girls begin puberty as young as 8 while others may not start until 15 years old.

It's OK if you start earlier or later. Your body will do what is right for you.

Some changes which

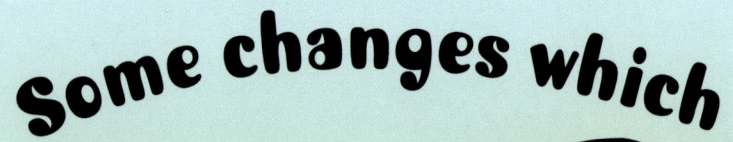

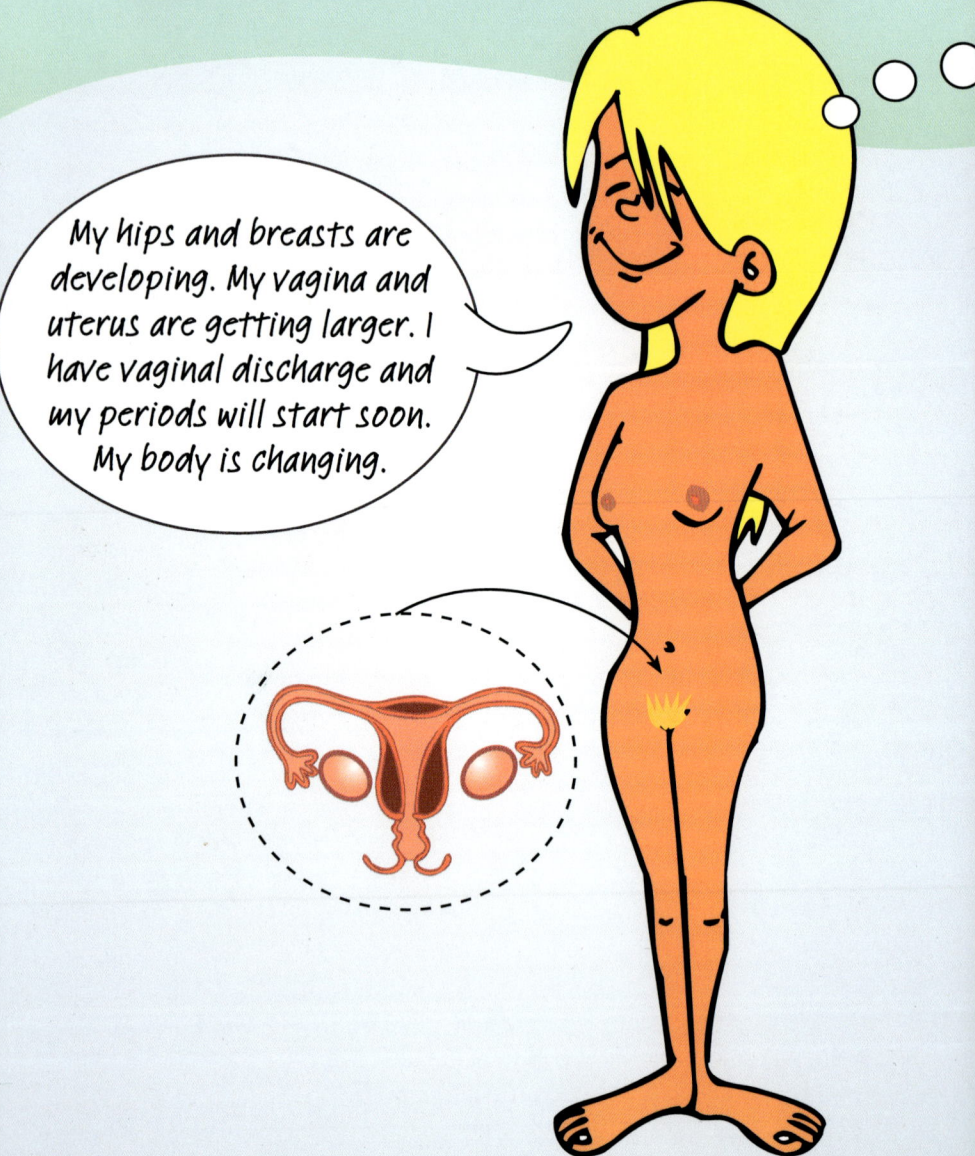

My hips and breasts are developing. My vagina and uterus are getting larger. I have vaginal discharge and my periods will start soon. My body is changing.

happen during puberty

I am growing taller, stronger and smarter. I am hungrier. I have body hair, pimples and BO. I have sexy feelings.

My penis and testicles are developing. I have erections. I have wet dreams.

Hormone levels change

At puberty a girl's body produces more female hormones.

The most important female hormones are oestrogen and progesterone. They are made in the ovaries.

Hormones contain chemical messages. They travel in the blood triggering the changes of puberty.

Puberty changes

- ♥ Body hair will start to grow.
- ♥ Hips and breasts develop.
- ♥ The vagina and uterus will get larger.
- ♥ Periods will start.

Every girl's body will change at different times and in different ways. Every girl will become taller, stronger and more curvy. Shapes will vary greatly. This is normal.

Hair in different places

Hair may grow
in funny places.
Round your nipples
on your faces.

In your undies,
tiny curls.
May start to grow
and surprise some girls.

On your legs
and under arms.
You may start
to feel alarmed.

But don't be worried,
don't be glum.
You'll grow up
gorgeous,
just like Mum!

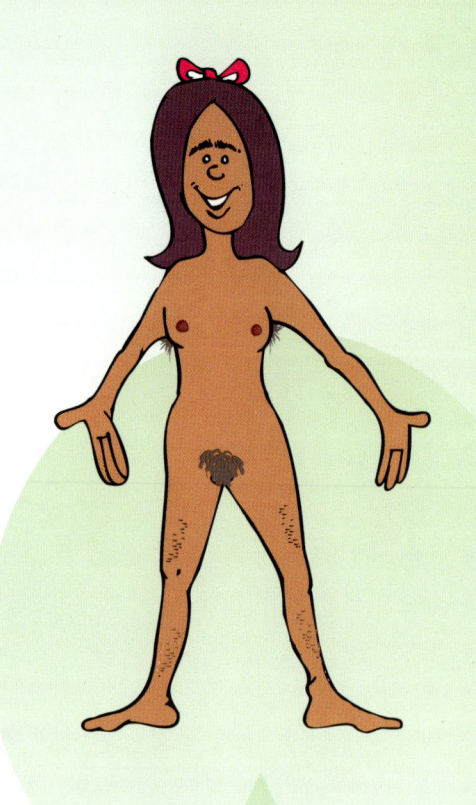

Body hair will increase gradually during puberty. Some girls will have very little and others will have more.

You may feel okay about your new body hair. Other girls may chose to remove hair on some parts of their body. Discuss what is right for you with a parent or carer.

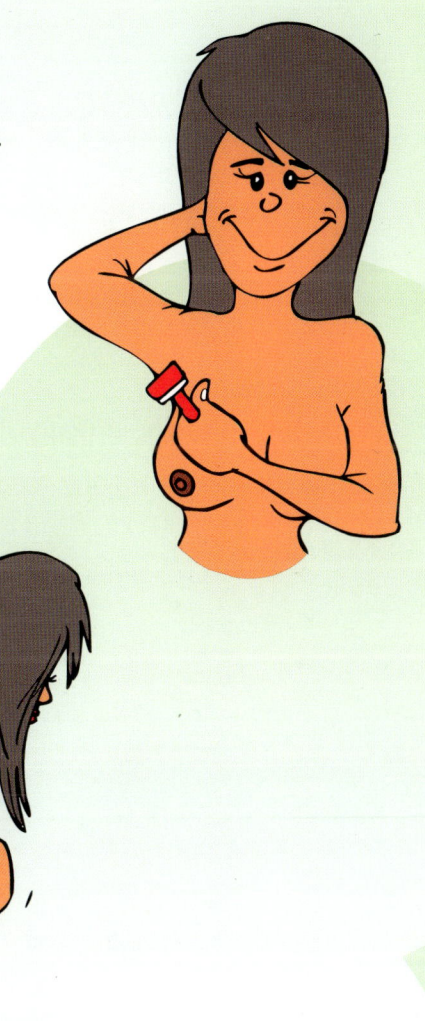

Pimples

At puberty, glands in the skin produce more oil. Pimples form when the oil glands become blocked and red.

You might be self-conscious about your pimples, but other people may hardly notice them.

Things which might help:

- Eat healthy food and drink lots of water
- Exercise regularly
- Wash your skin and hair regularly
- Always wash your face before you go to bed
- Brush or tie hair off the forehead
- Spend some time in the fresh air and sunshine every day

- Try not to touch pimples
- Pimple cream from the chemist
- Ask the doctor for advice
- If you have a special occasion, you can use concealer or make-up. Remember to wash it off carefully.

Smelling nice

Hormones make you sweat (perspire) more and your body odour becomes stronger.

Handy Hints

- Shower daily.
- Wash your vulva with water. Soap may irritate this sensitive skin.
- Shampoo your hair when it is oily.
- Apply deodorant.
- Wear clean underwear and socks every day.
- Change clothes and wear cotton socks for sport and other physical activities.

If your sneakers smell:
- Air them
- Change the inner sole
- Wash them carefully

Breasts

Breast development begins with a breast bud; a small lump behind the nipple.

Nipples become bigger. The area around the nipple, the areola, becomes darker.

Some girls have turned in or inverted nipples. This is normal.

Breasts grow bigger.

Breasts come in all shapes and sizes and that's OK.

At puberty, breasts can be tender, itchy or sensitive.

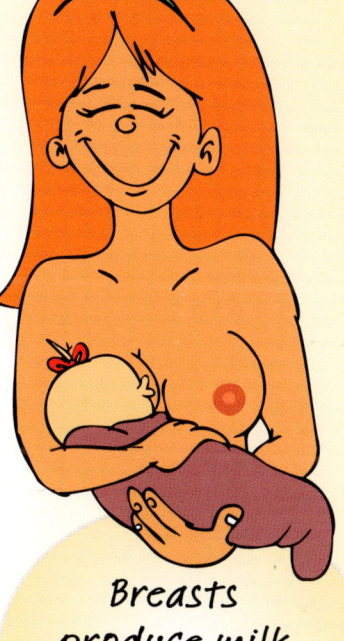

Breasts produce milk after a baby is born.

21

Checking breasts

Check your breasts as they grow and get to know what is normal for you. Before your period breasts can be tender and lumpy, so check them after your period.

See your doctor if you notice a change, or if you want to ask how to check your breasts thoroughly.

Bras and Camis

Breasts require support whether they are big or little.

Crop tops, camis, bras and sports bras are the answer.

Some girls can feel shy and embarrassed about their new shape while others are okay about it.

Whatever your new shape is, feel proud of it.

Changes down below

Female genitals are tucked away between your legs. They can't be easily seen.

You can have a look with a small mirror. If you separate the folds of skin with your fingers and look carefully, you can see small openings.

The correct name for this part of the body is the vulva. It is often called other things, for example the 'bottom', vagina or 'fanny'.

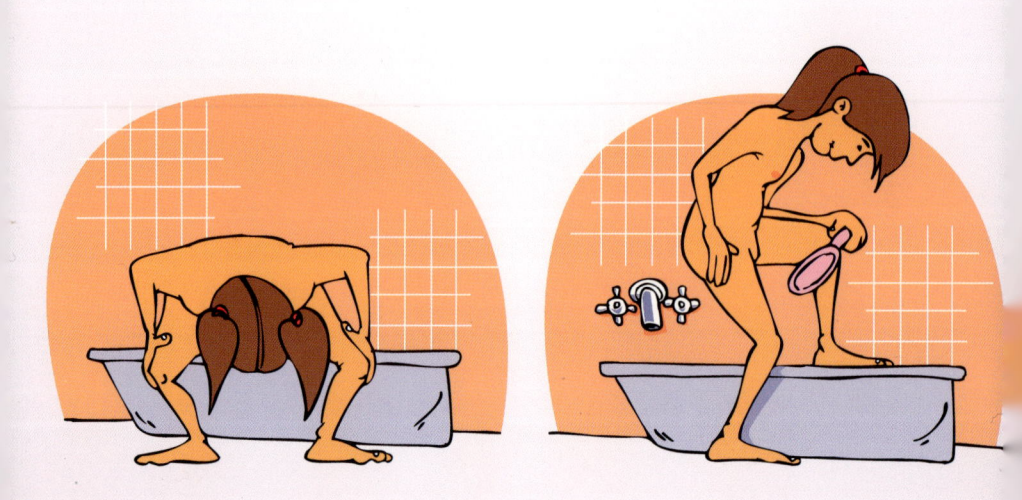

Looking at your vulva in a mirror

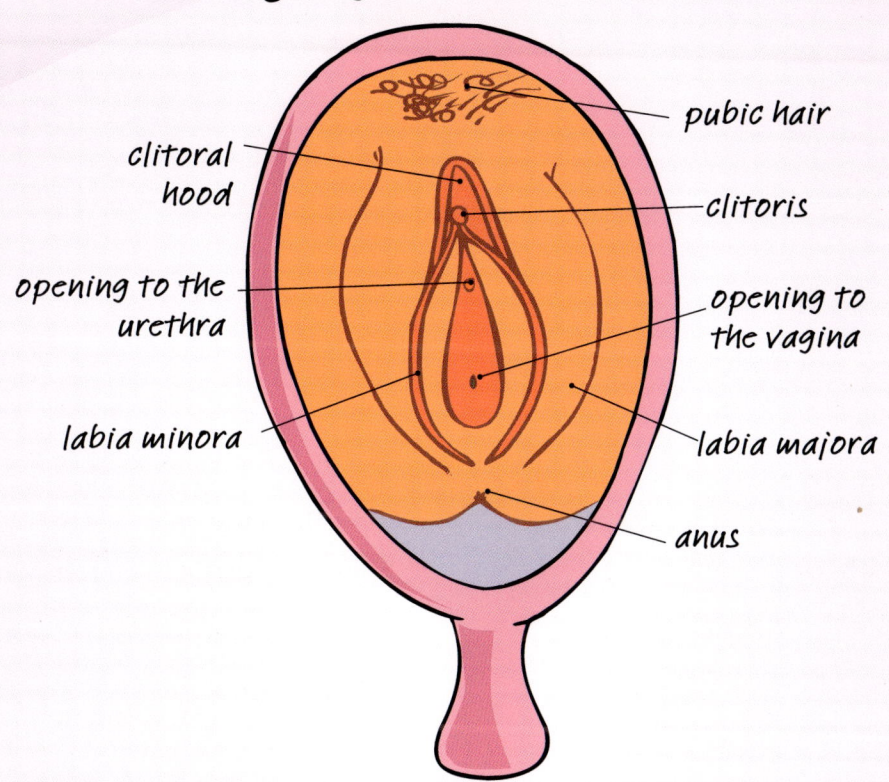

- pubic hair
- clitoral hood
- clitoris
- opening to the urethra
- opening to the vagina
- labia minora
- labia majora
- anus

Labia majora and labia minora – These folds of skin cover and protect the clitoris and openings to the urethra and vagina.

Clitoris (*pronounced* 'clit-er-us') – This is a small bump. It is the most sensitive part of the vulva. It is covered by a fold of skin or 'hood'.

Opening to the urethra – Opening of a narrow tube that leads to the bladder. Wee (urine) comes out here.

Anus – Poo (faeces) comes out here.

The female body parts needed to have a baby are inside the body. This is what you would see if you had special 'x-ray' glasses.

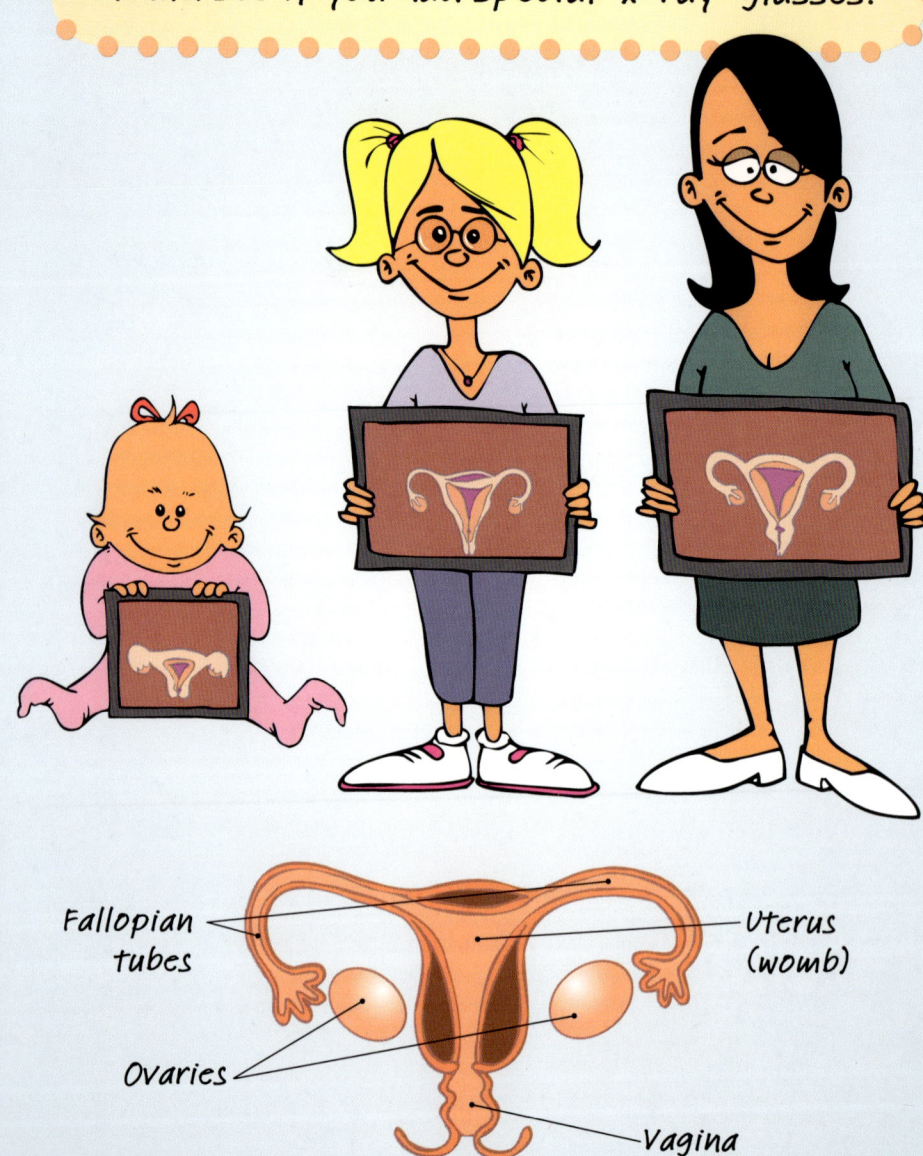

Fallopian tubes

Uterus (womb)

Ovaries

Vagina

Ovaries – By puberty, the ovaries have grown to the size of a walnut. Baby girls are born with thousands of tiny eggs which are stored in the ovaries. From puberty onwards, an egg ripens each month (ovulation) and pops out into the fallopian tube.

Fallopian tube – An egg travels along this narrow tube from the ovary to the uterus.

Uterus (womb) – The part of the body where the baby grows. It is the size and shape of a small pear.

Vagina – The vagina leads from the uterus to the outside of the body.

- Period blood comes out here.
- It is for sexual intercourse.
- It is the birth passage for a baby. It can stretch when a baby is born.

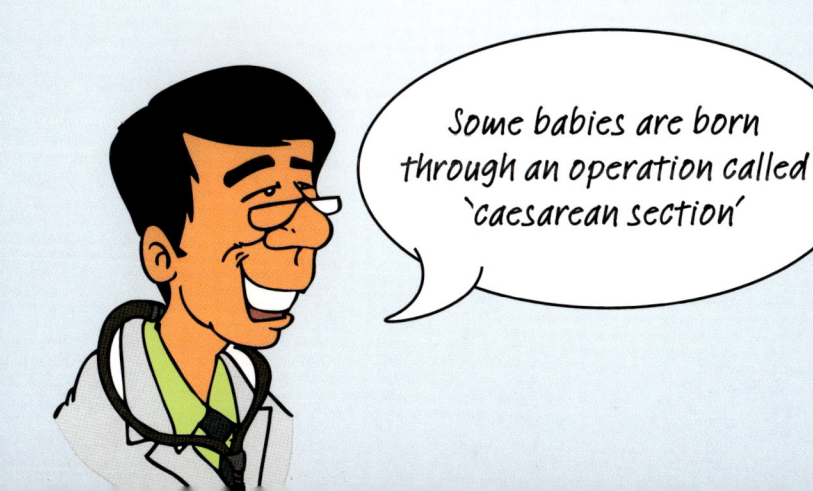

> Some babies are born through an operation called 'caesarean section'

How babies

A baby is made when an egg from a female joins with sperm from a male. This can happen as a result of sexual intercourse when a man's penis is in a woman's vagina. Their bodies move together and after a short time semen containing sperm comes out of the penis.

The sperm travels up through the uterus and into the fallopian tubes. If one strong sperm joins with an egg a baby begins to form.

The egg is very small, about the size of a 'full stop'.

Sperm are so small that you can only see them with a microscope.

are made

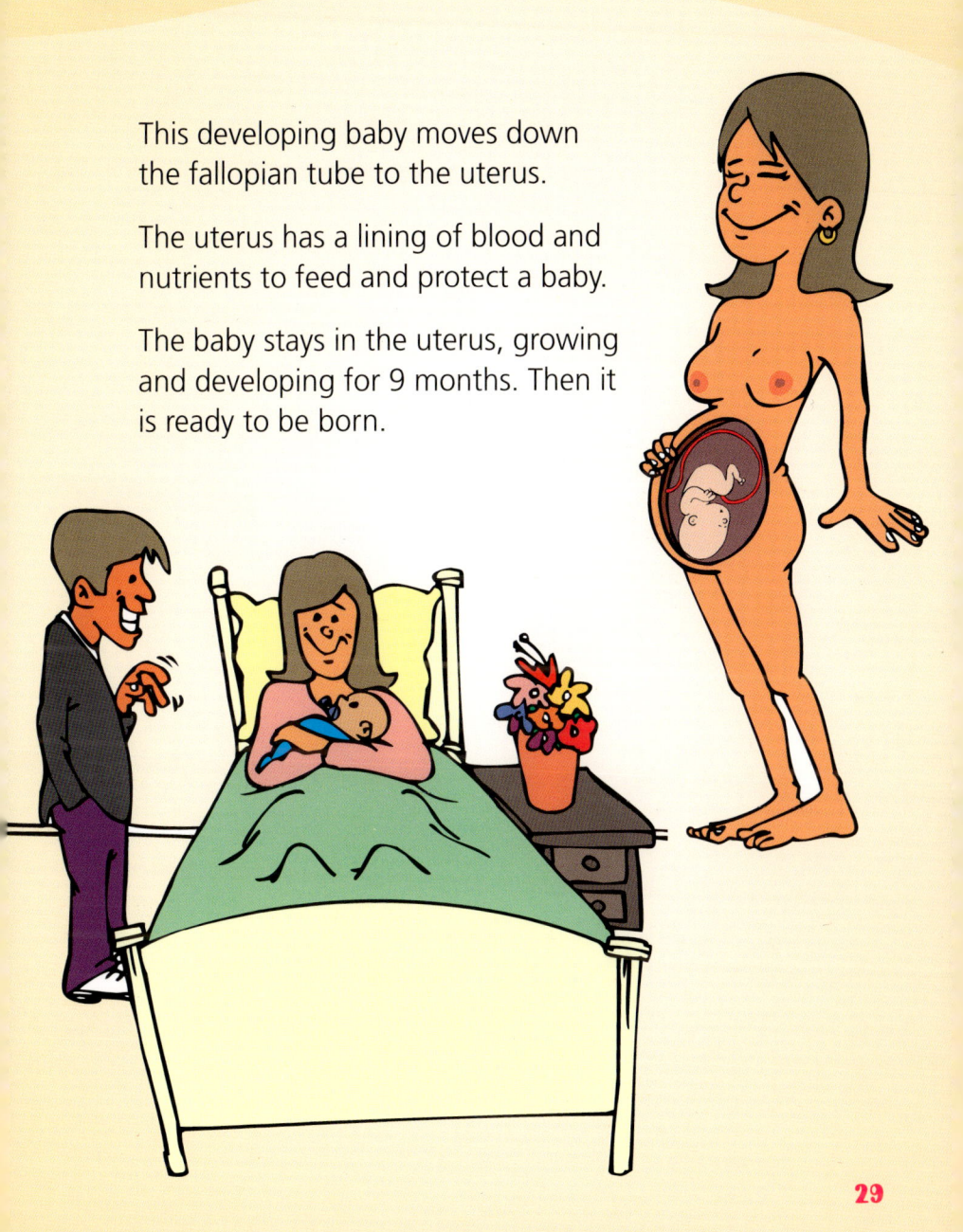

This developing baby moves down the fallopian tube to the uterus.

The uterus has a lining of blood and nutrients to feed and protect a baby.

The baby stays in the uterus, growing and developing for 9 months. Then it is ready to be born.

Why do girls

Every month the uterus makes a new lining of blood to feed and protect a baby if one is made. When a baby is not made, this lining dribbles slowly out of the vagina. This is called a period.

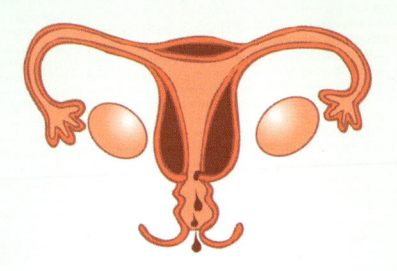

Approximately 2 weeks before your next period another egg will ripen and another lining will form in the uterus. If no baby is made, you get another period. This pattern is called your 'menstrual cycle'.

Usually you have a period each month. When you first start having periods, the time between periods can vary greatly. If you are worried, talk to your parent, carer or doctor.

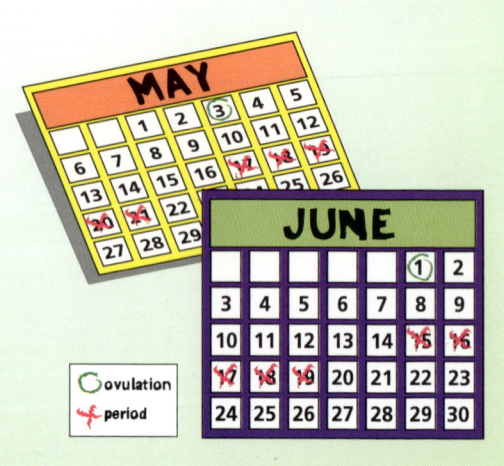

have periods?

This menstrual cycle continues until you are about 50 years old when you stop having periods. This is called menopause.

Some things which can change your menstrual cycle are:

- pregnancy
- medical reasons
- extreme exercise (olympic training)
- stress
- weight loss
- menopause.

There are many things which can change your menstrual cycle.

Signs that your period may start soon

Some puberty changes always happen before your periods begin. These changes are:

- pubic hair
- growth spurt
- underarm hair
- breast development
- mood swings
- vaginal discharge

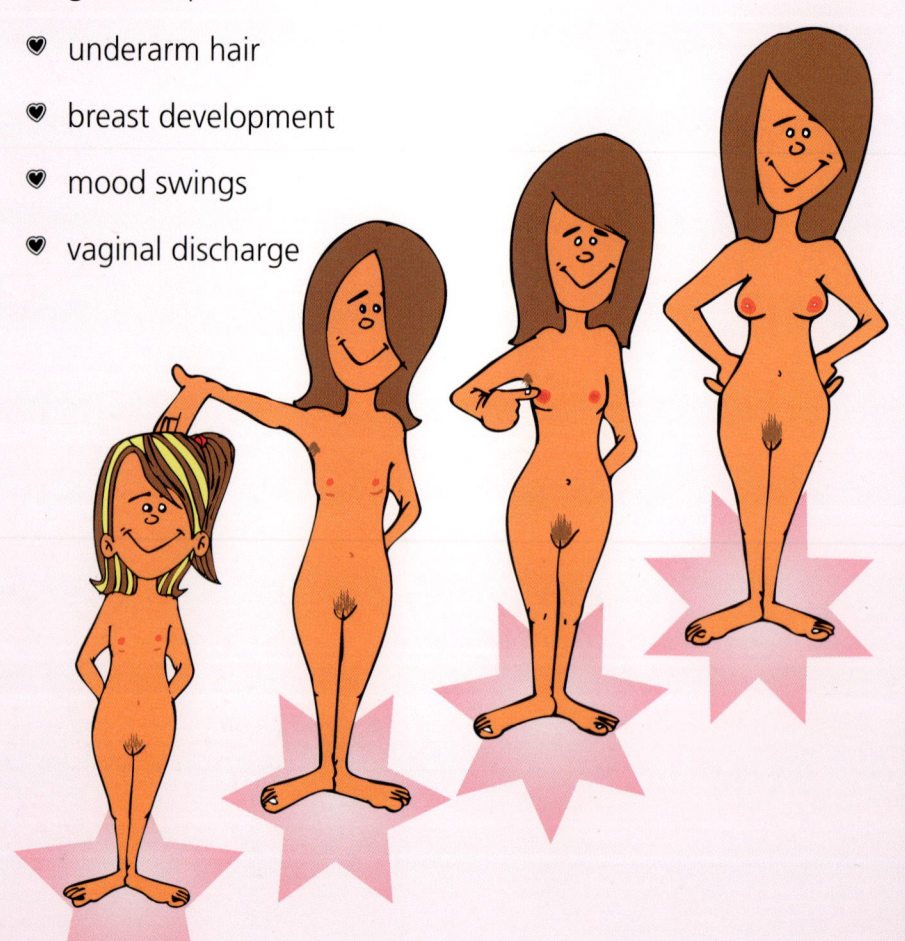

What is this wet white stuff?

This is vaginal discharge which comes from inside the vagina and keeps it moist. It is a small amount which can vary during your menstrual cycle from clear to white or cream in colour. The thickness changes as well. This is absolutely normal and healthy.

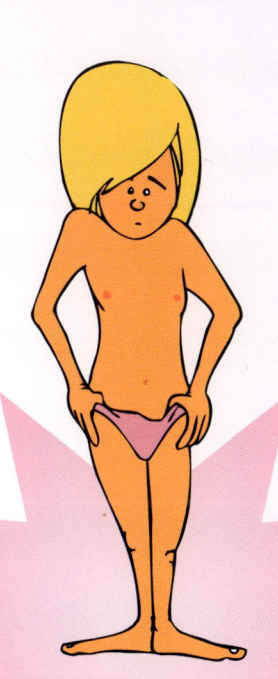

If you have an infection you may notice a change in the colour and smell of the discharge. Your vulva might feel itchy or sore. This is the time to see your doctor.

How will you know when you get your period?

You will have:
- A feeling of wetness around your vagina.
- A small amount of blood in your undies.

What is your period like?

It will last from 3–7 days.

There is more blood for the first few days then it slows down.

You will notice that the blood is a different colour from day to day.

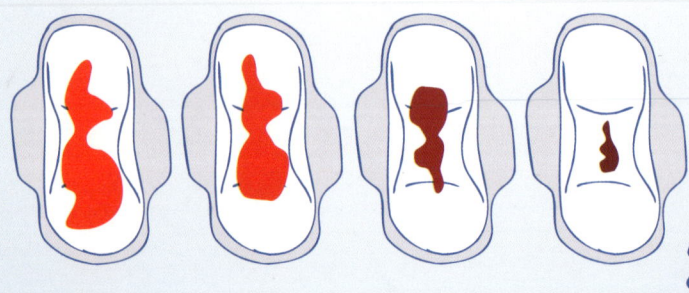

The amount of blood is small but can seem a lot.

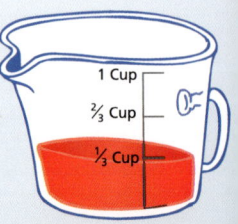

It is normal for blood to sometimes go on the undies, pyjamas or sheets.

If you have blood on your clothing or your sheet, soak it in cold water, then wash it.

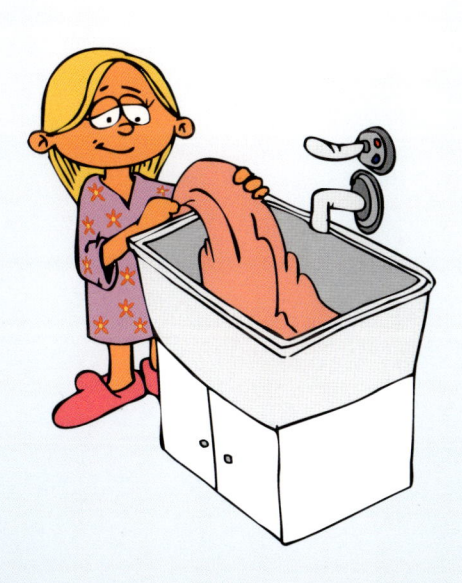

How will you feel around the time of your period?

You may be sensitive and get upset easily. You may be grumpy. You may feel a need for more privacy or a need for extra cuddles.

Your tummy may ache and feel bloated. Your breasts may be tender.

These feelings will soon disappear.

What can help?

Getting ready

When you have your period you will need some pads or tampons to absorb the blood.

It is a good idea to get ready before your period starts.

Pads and tampons can be bought at the supermarket, the chemist, the milk-bar or a service station.

Ask the person who cares for you to help.

Your period kit

Put in:
- 2 pads
- 2 paper bags
- spare undies
- plastic bag (for used undies)
- disposable wipes.

You can put them in a make-up purse or a small bag, ready for school or going out.

If mum and dad live separately, have some pads or tampons at both houses.

Use a calendar or diary to record the days you have your period. This will help you to plan.

A few days before your next period is due, take your period kit with you to school.

Using pads

Using pads is easy.

A pad has a sticky strip to stick inside the undies.

Pads come in different shapes and sizes. Thicker ones for heavy days (when you lose more blood), and thinner ones for lighter days. Check out which is best for you.

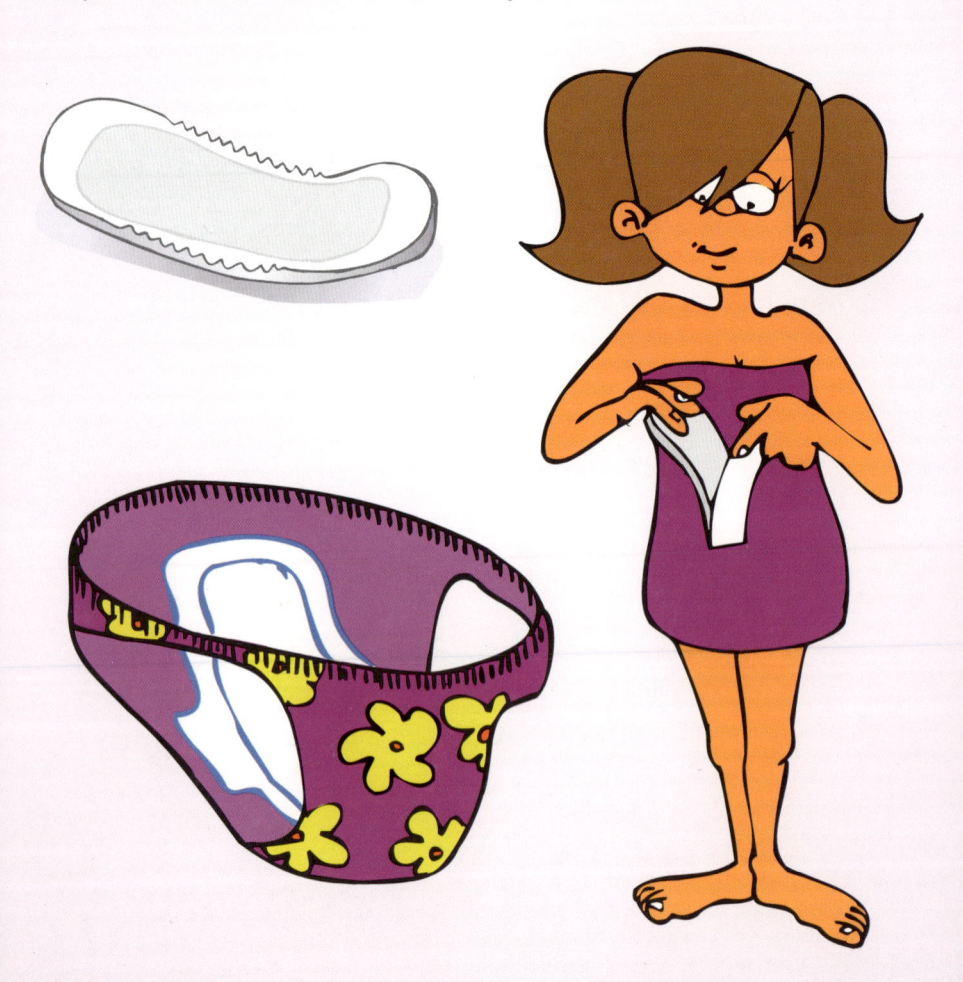

Changing pads

Pads need changing often. Some girls change every time they go to the toilet. If you wear a pad for more than 3 hours it can start to smell. Used pads should be wrapped and put in the bin.

Pads can't be flushed down the toilet.

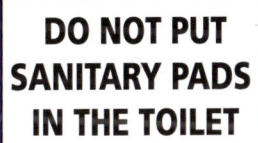

DO NOT PUT SANITARY PADS IN THE TOILET

Wash your hands after changing a pad.

About tampons

Tampons can be tricky at first, but with practice they are easy to use.

A tampon is about this size and can be carried in your pocket.

The tampon goes into the vagina and soaks up the blood before it dribbles out.

You can buy different sized tampons to suit your blood flow on different days. Use the smallest tampon to match your blood loss.

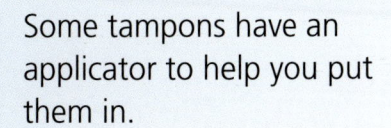

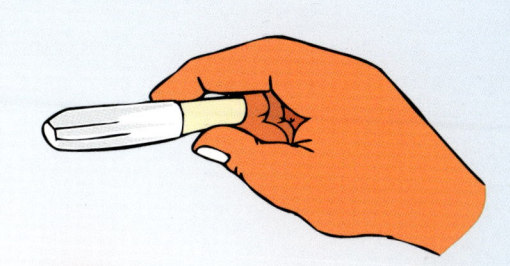

Some tampons have an applicator to help you put them in.

You must always wash your hands carefully before and after using tampons.

Tampons can be great for sport and swimming.

43

How to use a tampon

Remove the wrapper and uncurl the string.

Hold the tampon at the string end.

Lie on the bed, squat, or stand with one foot on the toilet.

Insert the rounded end into your vagina first and gently push the tampon right in.

You should not be able to feel it inside you. If it feels uncomfortable, the tampon might not be pushed in far enough.

Uterus

Bladder

Bowel

Vagina

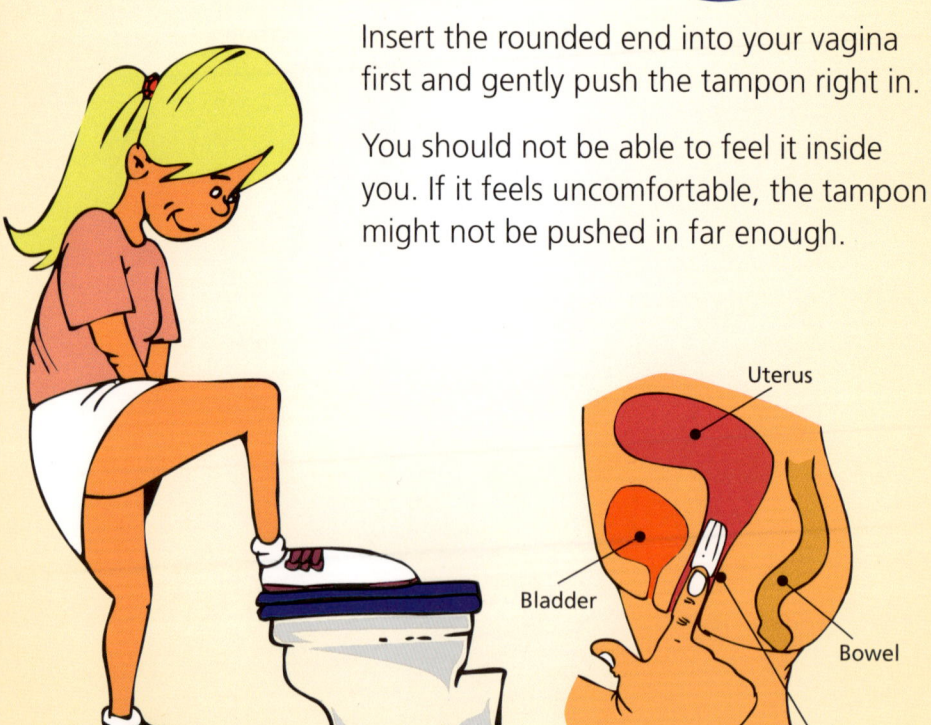

Changing tampons

Tampons need to be changed when they are full of blood. They should not be left in the vagina for more than 4 hours.

To remove the tampon, gently pull it out with the string.

PLEASE PUT SANITARY PRODUCTS IN THE SPECIAL BIN PROVIDED

Wrap the used tampon in paper. Put it in the rubbish bin or in a special sanitary bin if one is available.

Do not flush them down the toilet.

45

Mood swings

At puberty, hormones not only change the way our bodies look and work, they also change the way we think and feel.

Your feelings may change quickly. You might find yourself:

- Feeling misunderstood.
- Arguing with family, teachers or friends.
- Wanting to be by yourself.
- Feeling angry.
- Sad, or crying.
- Feeling lonely.

This is not much fun!

But also you might be:
- ♥ Having a fabulous time with friends.
- ♥ Very energetic.
- ♥ Telling great jokes.
- ♥ Thoughtful and supportive of others.
- ♥ Increasingly independent.
- ♥ More responsible.
- ♥ Trusted to make choices.

Talk about your feelings

It is normal to feel sad or angry at times, but if these feelings don't improve, you need to talk to your family, your teacher, a counsellor or a doctor.

♥ These things might help

If you are feeling out of sorts, upset or angry then these things might help:

Exercise

- ♥ dancing
- ♥ swimming
- ♥ jogging
- ♥ walking the dog
- ♥ bike riding

Have some quiet time by yourself

- ♥ Read a book.
- ♥ Paint or draw.
- ♥ Take a bath.
- ♥ Listen to music.
- ♥ Write a journal.
- ♥ Do relaxation exercises.
- ♥ Count slowly from 1 to 10.
- ♥ Do some calm, deep breathing.

Spend some time with your family or friends.

Think more helpful thoughts

Change from negative thinking to positive thinking.

Plan an activity or a special treat for yourself.

This is awful. I can't stand it

I can stand it. I can do lots of things to help myself feel better.

Friends, boyfriends,

At puberty it is normal for girls to become more aware of boys and think a lot about having a boyfriend.

Blushing can be embarrassing for some girls. Their face goes red and they feel hot and sweaty when they talk to boys.

girlfriends

Thinking about love and sex is something that happens a lot from puberty onwards.

Many girls find that during puberty they think about one particular person in this way. This is called a crush.

You might have a crush on someone with whom you would not expect to have a romantic relationship.

If a girl has a crush on another girl or woman this does not necessarily mean she is gay. However a few girls are naturally same sex attracted. This can be a confusing and worrying time for a while.

Private moments

From the time they are babies girls may touch or rub their vulva when they are naked. This might be when they are having their nappy changed, or in the bath. This is normal.

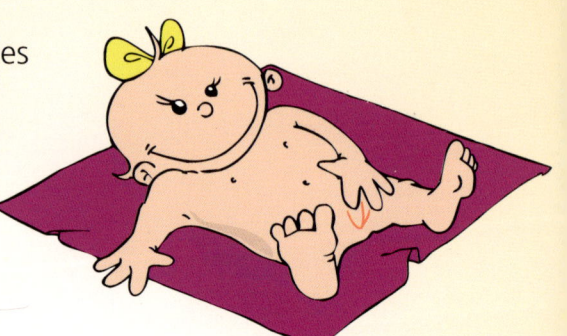

Some girls may hold or touch this area when they have clothes on. It may give them a nice comfortable feeling.

At puberty, the body produces more hormones, which causes an increase in sexy feelings. These are warm, tingly feelings in the nipples, vulva and vagina. When girls or women have sexy thoughts, their nipples may become harder. Their vagina and vulva may become moist.

Masturbation

Some girls may choose to masturbate when they have sexy feelings. This should be done in private.

Masturbation is a way for girls and young women to discover how their body feels and works. This is part of normal development.

Masturbation is touching or rubbing the vulva and clitoris. This may give very pleasant enjoyable feelings. If you continue to rub and touch your clitoris and vulva you might have an orgasm.

An orgasm is a really nice warm tingly feeling around this area. It is a very strong feeling for a moment, then it fades. This leaves you with a warm relaxed feeling.

Some girls will masturbate early in puberty, some later. Some girls will not feel comfortable exploring their body in this way.

Your Body... Your Rights

Our bodies are private.

We have the right to decide who can see or touch our bodies.

There are very few times when another person will need to look at or touch your private parts. One example would be if you need a medical check.

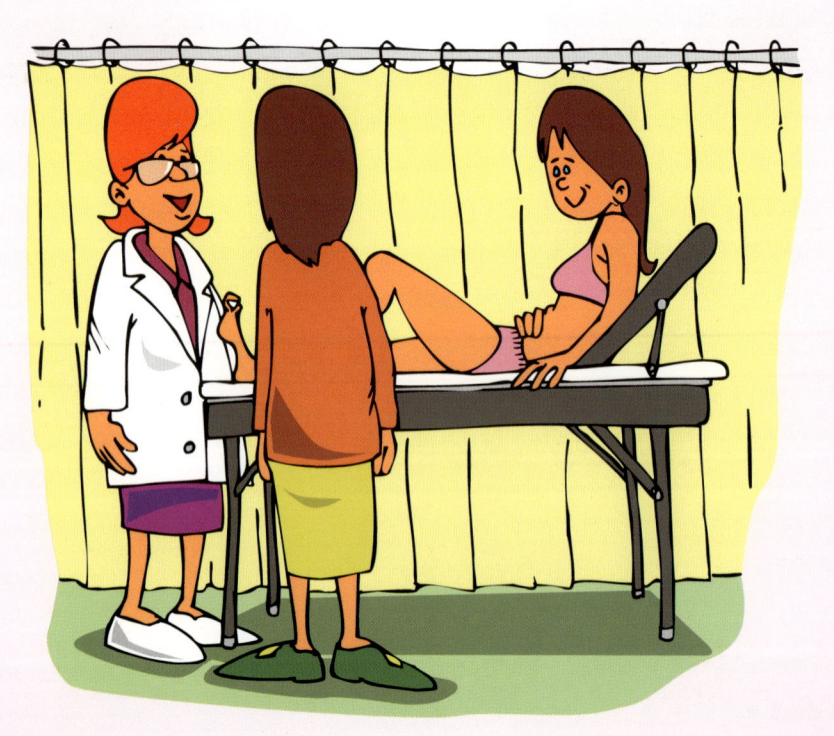

This is an important message about touching that is "NOT OKAY"

If someone looks at or touches your body in a way that makes you feel uncomfortable, this could be sexual abuse.

If sexual abuse happens to you, it is NOT your fault. Don't keep it a secret! Tell an adult you can trust, as soon as you can.

Feeling good

Lots of girls worry about how they look. This is normal, but not helpful.

Bodies come in many different shapes and sizes and change at different ages.

Body shape and size are influenced by our 'genes' which come to us from our mother's egg and father's sperm. These genes are mixed up to give each baby a new, unique combination.

Many girls worry about their weight. There is a wide range of healthy weight depending on age, height and body type. You can check with your doctor to see what is right for you.

about your body

By eating healthy food, having enough sleep and taking regular exercise our bodies will be the best they can be. This will make us feel good.

Remember, whatever your body shape, you can have great friendships, be happy and healthy.

Looking your best

Some tips for looking gorgeous!

Posture

Stand straight and tall.

Check posture: tummy in, shoulders back, head up.

Clothes

Talk to mum and shop assistants about clothes that fit you well and suit your body shape.

Whatever your body shape, dress to look gorgeous!

Hair

Clean, shiny hair always looks good.

Experiment with different styles to see what suits you.

Ask the hairdresser which cut will suit your hair.

Make-up

If you are using make-up, keep it light and natural-looking.

Talk to the sales assistant in the chemist about different products.

Nails

Keep your nails clean and well shaped.

You might like to try natural-coloured nail polish.

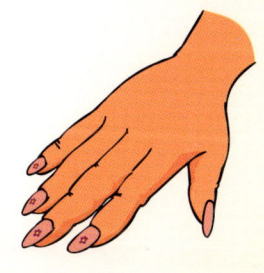

It is important to feel good about your body and have a positive attitude about your appearance.

In this book you have learnt that you will experience many changes during your journey through puberty.

Some of these may be embarrassing or uncomfortable for a while.

However there are lots of exciting and positive things that are happening.

ENJOY!

On the next few pages there are hints for mums, dads, and other significant adults.

Hints for mums, dads, and

Forward planning

- Read *More Secret Girls' Business®* a few times, becoming comfortable with the vocabulary and subject matter.
- Think carefully about how you will use the book, and how you will present it to your daughter. Which topics will you follow-up with her?
- Your reaction to your daughter's changes will have a lasting impression on her confidence and self esteem.
- A positive attitude towards growth and change will empower girls to become confident young women.

Vocabulary

- Families often develop their own language for private body parts and functions. It is important for girls to know correct names and appropriate language for different situations, such as talking to the doctor.
- Encourage your daughter to become confident in communicating with the doctor. When she is a little older, she will be able to make appointments independently to talk about private matters.
- It is good for girls to understand the changes boys experience at puberty and to have appropriate vocabulary. See *Secret Boys' Business®* also in this series.

other significant adults

When to talk about puberty changes

- Parents can talk about differences between boys and girls, how babies are made, and body changes from the time children are very young. Don't wait until puberty to talk about these things.

- Discussion about puberty needs to be part of everyday communication and not a 'one off' chat.

- When puberty is imminent, more specific discussion can take place about body changes.

- Keep the lines of communication open and be prepared to discuss any queries or comments in a thoughtful way.

- If questions are asked at awkward moments, say that you will talk about it later in private. Be certain to follow up as soon as possible.

Getting ready for periods

- Before your daughter has her first period make sure she has her period kit ready.

- Talk about what it might be like to have a period before it happens. It's okay to share your experiences in a positive way.

- Ensure there are always plenty of pads and paper bags in the house for your daughter to use.

- Make sure your daughter knows how to dispose of used pads, and have a rubbish bin close to the toilet.

- Girls who begin puberty earlier than their peers may feel embarrassed about their body changes and awkward about period management.

- All girls undergoing changes at puberty will have self-conscious moments.

- Encourage siblings to be respectful about puberty changes and not to embarrass, joke or tease.

Keeping track

- Encourage your daughter to keep a menstrual diary or calendar.

- Be aware of your daughter's mood changes around the time of her period. This will help keep things calm. You may need to back off and be a bit gentle.

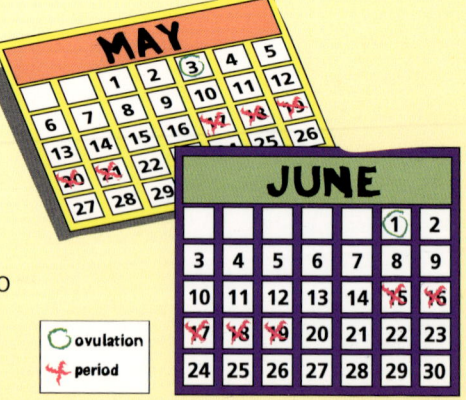

Healthy bodies, healthy self- esteem

- Young women take on board messages they see and hear about weight and body shape. If your daughter is present, avoid discussing personal weight issues or being critical of your own body shape.
- Be aware of messages about body image in the media and discuss these with your daughter.
- Value your daughter's positive qualities, and take care to avoid negative comments about her body shape.
- Model healthy living, eating and exercising.
- Ensure there is a range of nutritious foods available for snacks and prepare healthy meals.
- Encourage water instead of sugary drinks.
- Establish a regular sleep routine ensuring adequate sleep each night.
- Exercise should be a regular part of the daily routine.

Feelings

- Listen carefully to your daughter when she is talking about her worries. Acknowledge and validate her feelings.
- Don't feel that you have to take responsibility for solving her problems. It is more helpful to coach her to problem-solve, discussing possible courses of action and their outcomes.

Friends, boyfriends and girlfriends

- It is normal to have friends who are girls and friends who are boys. Reinforce with girls that this is normal and different from a romantic relationship.
- Taunts about boyfriend/girlfriend relationships make many girls uncomfortable and can be a form of bullying. If this becomes a problem, discuss it with her teacher.
- *The Secret Business of Relationships, Love and Sex*™ book has fantastic information about teenage relationships.

Same sex attraction

- Some girls wonder or worry if they are 'same-sex attracted'. It is important that adults do not give negative messages about sexual orientation.
- If you need advice about same sex attraction contact your local Family Planning Association

Privacy – A very important issue

- At puberty there is a need for more privacy in the home. Family members should knock and wait for acknowledgement before entering bathrooms or bedrooms which are occupied.
- Parents' reaction to masturbation can have lasting effects on a girl's self-esteem and sexuality. Negative reactions are not helpful. Respect her privacy!

Protective behaviours – personal safety

- Discuss appropriate sexual behaviour, what is okay and what is not.
- Be aware that girls can be sexually abused.
- Girls need to know what to do and who to tell if they experience inappropriate sexual behaviour.
- If your daughter tells you about sexual abuse, remain calm, believe her, and never blame. Protect her from further abuse.
- Any concerns can be discussed with your local CASA (Centre Against Sexual Assault).
- There is a lot of inappropriate sexual information on the internet. Discuss this with girls and monitor internet use.

If sexual abuse happens to you, it is NOT your fault. Don't keep it a secret! Tell an adult you can trust, as soon as you can.

Specially for dads and their daughters

- Dads can support their daughters by reading this book and discussing the contents.
- It is important for fathers to model respect for privacy. Knock and wait for permission before entering your daughter's bedroom or the bathroom.
- Acknowledge to your daughter that periods are a normal part of a woman's life. This will be a reassuring, positive message for her.
- Make sure that your daughter understands that it is okay to talk about periods when you are around. This will reduce possible awkwardness and embarrassment about this topic.
- When planning trips in the car allow regular toilet stops so pads or tampons can be changed.
- Help other siblings, including brothers, to understand about periods and be respectful.

- Be prepared to include pads or tampons on the shopping list.
- Be aware that girls may be teary, oversensitive and out of sorts around the time of their period. Back off and be sensitive and considerate at this time.
- Be prepared to be involved and supportive, particularly if her mother is not around.
- Sometimes girls living or staying with their fathers may need a female adult friend to help with puberty issues such as periods and bras.
- For some girls, their relationship with Dad can change suddenly at puberty. Girls may become less comfortable with physical closeness to their father. They may chose to spend less time with Dad and the family, and more time with friends. Your daughter will develop her own interests, attitudes and opinions, becoming more independent in her thinking. This is an essential part of growing up.
- Be proud! Your daughter is on the way to becoming a young woman!

Books written and published by
Secret Girls' Business®

Please visit us at www.secretgb.com or email at secretgb@hotmail.com